Through the Letters of
Come Millenniums of Ottawa

M. Bordone

by Velma Seawell Daniels

The C.R. Gibson Company, Norwalk, CT 06856

Published by The C.R. Gibson Company,
Norwalk, Connecticut 06856

ISBN 0-8378-2531-8
GB552

Anniversary Symbols

First — paper
Second — cotton, calico
Third — leather
Fourth — fruit, flowers, books, (silk, linen)
Fifth — wood
Sixth — candy, sugar, iron
Seventh — wool, copper, brass, bronze
Eighth — rubber, electrical appliances, (bronze, pottery)
Ninth — pottery, willow, china
Tenth — tin, aluminum
Eleventh — steel
Twelfth — linen, silk, nylon
Thirteenth — lace
Fourteenth — ivory
Fifteenth — crystal
Twentieth — china
Twenty-fifth — silver
Thirtieth — pearl
Thirty-fifth — coral, jade
Fortieth — ruby
Forty-fifth — sapphire
Fiftieth — golden
Fifty-fifth — emerald
Seventy-fifth — diamond

*T*he holiest of all holidays are those
Kept by ourselves in silence and apart;
The secret anniversaries of the heart.

Henry Wadsworth Longfellow

*H*appy Anniversary! My greeting card on the breakfast table was simple; just a sheet of note paper folded in the middle like a tiny tent. With a red felt pen, my husband had drawn a heart and written these words. "It's on the back porch."

Like a kid, with my husband right behind me, I rushed out the back door, not even taking time for my orange juice.

There stood a concrete bird bath, about three feet tall, the kind you can find at most garden supply shops. A potted plant, a foot or two taller, stood beside it. In the bowl of the birdbath was a box of sugar and a dozen or so of those colorful little things that are used to scrub pots and pans which some people call "pot-scratchers."

"Wonderful," I shouted. (It had to be, of course, because everything he does is wonderful). "But what's it all about?"

"It's like this," he said. "Because you spend most of your time at the typewriter in the study, I'm going to plant this bush just outside the window. Beside the bush goes the birdbath and the pot scratchers go in that. We'll fill it with sugar water to attract butterflies. The plant is called a buddleia or a butterfly bush."

Well, the butterfly bush blossomed and the butterflies come to feed from the nectar of its purple flowers. Others perch on the pot scratchers and drink sugar water.

How great the hand of God! I watch a butterfly as it emerges from its cocoon and through all the wonderful stages of its life and I think God meant for us to blossom with each new stage of our life.

Sometimes when I see my tiny little friends outside my window, they bring to mind the words of Browning's Rabbi ben Ezra, "Grow old along with me, the best is yet to be."

The anniversary party would go down as the social event of the season. More than 250 guests moved in and out of the living room, the parlor, the library, the family room, the den, upstairs, downstairs, the pool-side house and a dozen secluded nooks on the four-acre estate. Plenty of food and drink available.

The charming guest of honor, with an empty glass in her hand, approached the hostess and said, "Excuse me, but could you tell me where to find that cute little dark haired girl wearing the ballet tu-tu who was serving drinks?"

"Oh," said the hostess, "you're looking for a drink?"

"No," the guest said, I'm looking for my husband."

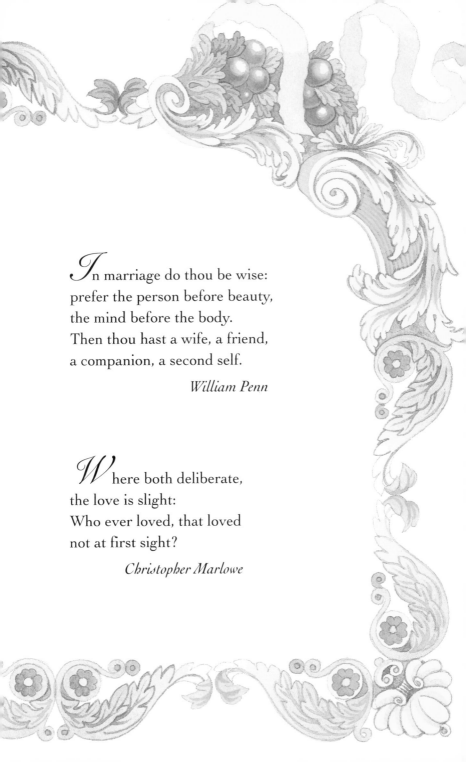

*I*n marriage do thou be wise:
prefer the person before beauty,
the mind before the body.
Then thou hast a wife, a friend,
a companion, a second self.

William Penn

*W*here both deliberate,
the love is slight:
Who ever loved, that loved
not at first sight?

Christopher Marlowe

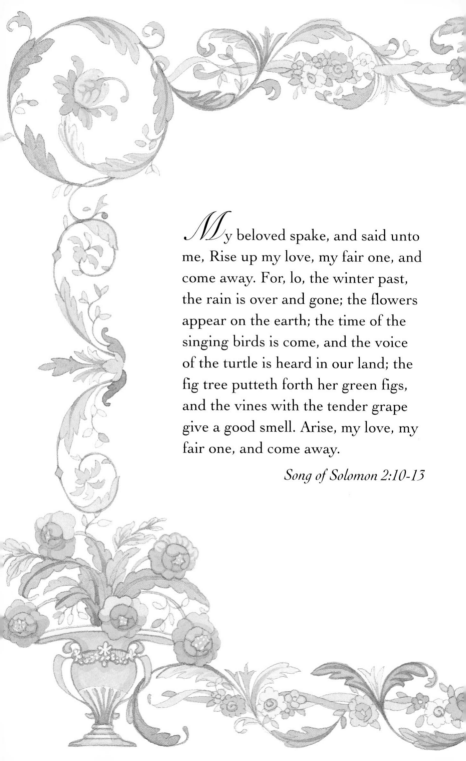

*M*y beloved spake, and said unto me, Rise up my love, my fair one, and come away. For, lo, the winter past, the rain is over and gone; the flowers appear on the earth; the time of the singing birds is come, and the voice of the turtle is heard in our land; the fig tree putteth forth her green figs, and the vines with the tender grape give a good smell. Arise, my love, my fair one, and come away.

Song of Solomon 2:10-13

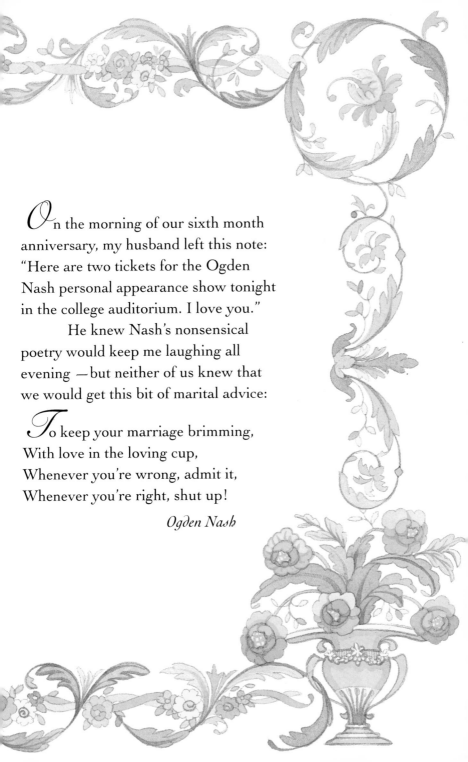

*O*n the morning of our sixth month anniversary, my husband left this note: "Here are two tickets for the Ogden Nash personal appearance show tonight in the college auditorium. I love you."

He knew Nash's nonsensical poetry would keep me laughing all evening —but neither of us knew that we would get this bit of marital advice:

*T*o keep your marriage brimming,
With love in the loving cup,
Whenever you're wrong, admit it,
Whenever you're right, shut up!

Ogden Nash

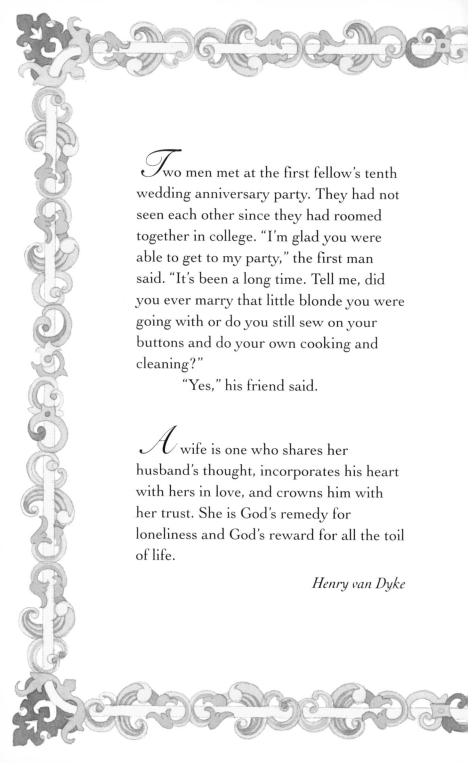

*T*wo men met at the first fellow's tenth wedding anniversary party. They had not seen each other since they had roomed together in college. "I'm glad you were able to get to my party," the first man said. "It's been a long time. Tell me, did you ever marry that little blonde you were going with or do you still sew on your buttons and do your own cooking and cleaning?"

"Yes," his friend said.

A wife is one who shares her husband's thought, incorporates his heart with hers in love, and crowns him with her trust. She is God's remedy for loneliness and God's reward for all the toil of life.

Henry van Dyke

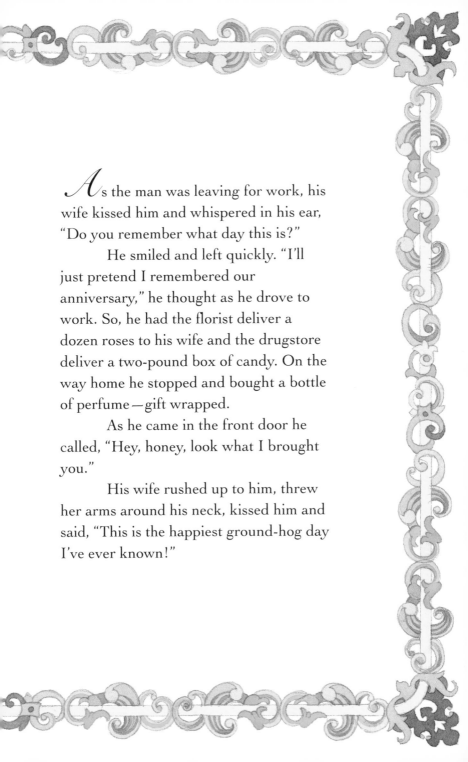

As the man was leaving for work, his wife kissed him and whispered in his ear, "Do you remember what day this is?"

He smiled and left quickly. "I'll just pretend I remembered our anniversary," he thought as he drove to work. So, he had the florist deliver a dozen roses to his wife and the drugstore deliver a two-pound box of candy. On the way home he stopped and bought a bottle of perfume—gift wrapped.

As he came in the front door he called, "Hey, honey, look what I brought you."

His wife rushed up to him, threw her arms around his neck, kissed him and said, "This is the happiest ground-hog day I've ever known!"

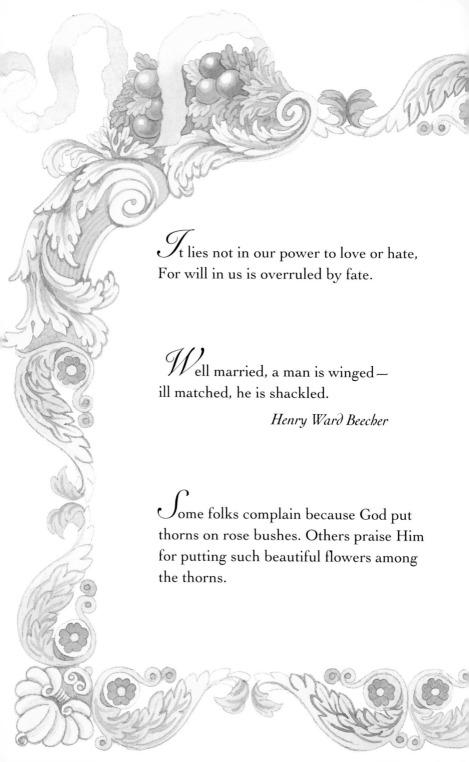

It lies not in our power to love or hate,
For will in us is overruled by fate.

Well married, a man is winged —
ill matched, he is shackled.

Henry Ward Beecher

Some folks complain because God put
thorns on rose bushes. Others praise Him
for putting such beautiful flowers among
the thorns.

The young man finally spoke to his girlfriend's father about marrying his daughter.

"I know it's a mere formality," the young man said, "but we thought you would be pleased if I asked."

"Just where did you get the idea," her father asked, "that asking my consent to the marriage was a mere formality?"

"From your wife," the young man said.

$\mathcal{O}$my luve is like a red, red rose,
That's newly sprung in June:
O my luve is like the melodie
That's sweetly played in tune.
As fair art thou, my bonnie lass,
So deep in luve am I;
And I will luve thee still, my dear,
Till a' the seas gang dry.
Till a' the seas gang dry, my dear,
And the rocks melt wi' the sun:
And I will luve thee still, my dear,
While the sands o' life shall run.
And fare thee weel, my only luve!
And fare thee weel a while!
And I will come again, my luve,
Tho' it were ten thousand mile.

Robert Burns

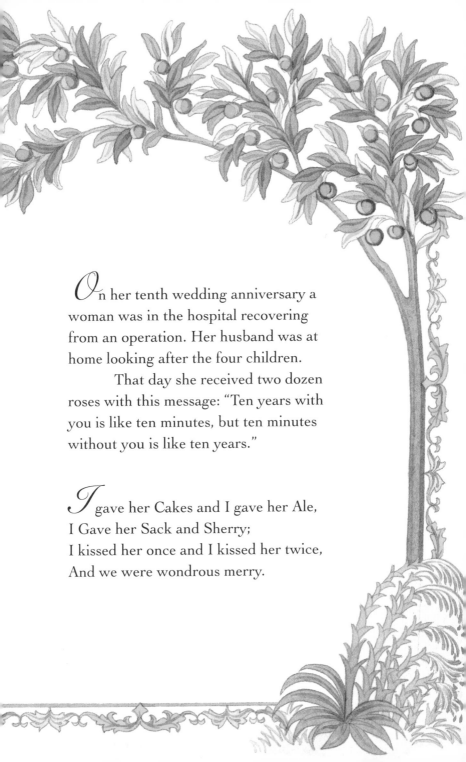

On her tenth wedding anniversary a
woman was in the hospital recovering
from an operation. Her husband was at
home looking after the four children.

     That day she received two dozen
roses with this message: "Ten years with
you is like ten minutes, but ten minutes
without you is like ten years."

I gave her Cakes and I gave her Ale,
I Gave her Sack and Sherry;
I kissed her once and I kissed her twice,
And we were wondrous merry.

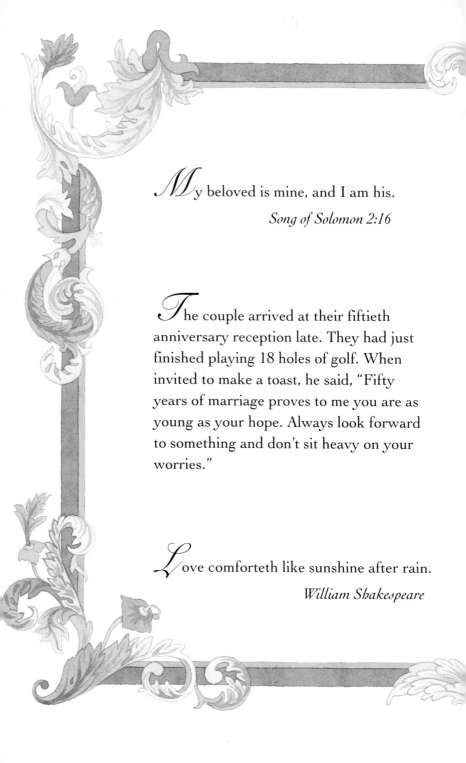

My beloved is mine, and I am his.

Song of Solomon 2:16

The couple arrived at their fiftieth anniversary reception late. They had just finished playing 18 holes of golf. When invited to make a toast, he said, "Fifty years of marriage proves to me you are as young as your hope. Always look forward to something and don't sit heavy on your worries."

Love comforteth like sunshine after rain.

William Shakespeare

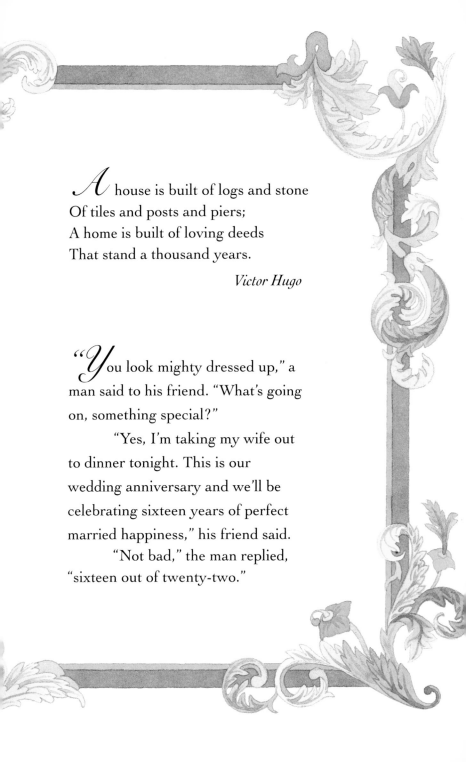

A house is built of logs and stone
Of tiles and posts and piers;
A home is built of loving deeds
That stand a thousand years.

Victor Hugo

"You look mighty dressed up," a man said to his friend. "What's going on, something special?"

"Yes, I'm taking my wife out to dinner tonight. This is our wedding anniversary and we'll be celebrating sixteen years of perfect married happiness," his friend said.

"Not bad," the man replied, "sixteen out of twenty-two."

*G*rief can take care of itself, but to get the full value of joy you must have somebody to divide it with.

Mark Twain

*T*here is no more lovely, friendly and charming relationship, communion or company than a good marriage.

Martin Luther

A smile between husband and wife is a silent way of saying, "I love you."

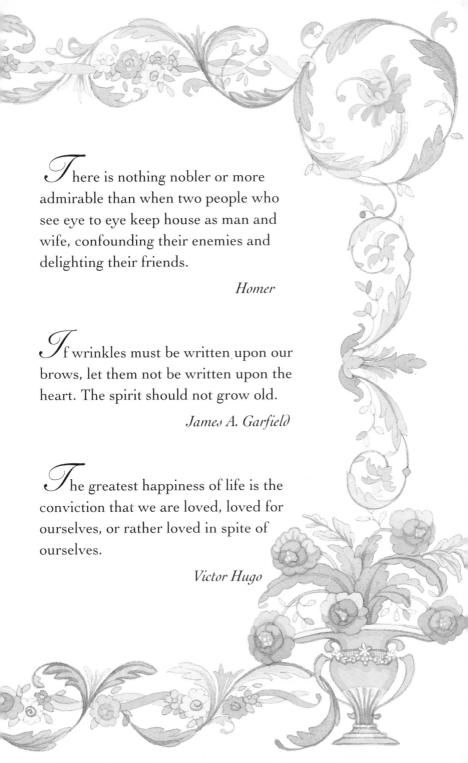

There is nothing nobler or more admirable than when two people who see eye to eye keep house as man and wife, confounding their enemies and delighting their friends.

Homer

If wrinkles must be written upon our brows, let them not be written upon the heart. The spirit should not grow old.

James A. Garfield

The greatest happiness of life is the conviction that we are loved, loved for ourselves, or rather loved in spite of ourselves.

Victor Hugo

We were guests at our friend's sixtieth wedding anniversary party. When it came time for toasts, the little gray-haired great-grandmother, the star of the evening, was called on to say something.

"Tell us your secret for a long and happy marriage," someone called out.

With a twinkle in her eye she said, "When we were married sixty years ago, an aunt in Ashtabula gave me some good advice. She said that to keep arguments from developing, my husband and I should do things together. She said, for example, I should weed the vegetable garden with my husband, and that I should listen to the ball games on radio with him, and that he should go grocery shopping with me.

Well, none of those things worked out. We didn't have a vegetable garden, and I hated baseball on the radio and he refused to set foot in the grocery store. But, I did find one thing we could do together. Whenever we got into a serious argument, I always helped settle it by mopping up the kitchen floor with him."

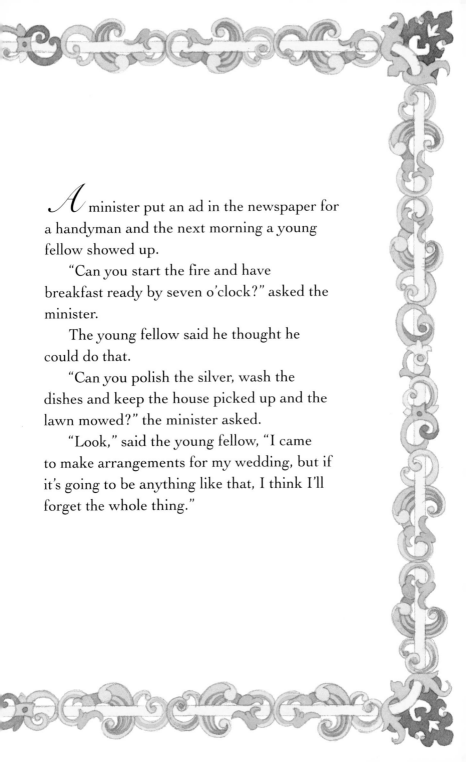

$\mathcal{A}$ minister put an ad in the newspaper for a handyman and the next morning a young fellow showed up.

"Can you start the fire and have breakfast ready by seven o'clock?" asked the minister.

The young fellow said he thought he could do that.

"Can you polish the silver, wash the dishes and keep the house picked up and the lawn mowed?" the minister asked.

"Look," said the young fellow, "I came to make arrangements for my wedding, but if it's going to be anything like that, I think I'll forget the whole thing."

$\mathcal{L}$ove seems the swiftest, but it is the slowest of all growths. No man or woman really knows what perfect love is until they have been married a quarter of a century.

Mark Twain

$\mathcal{I}$ will tell you, scholar, I have heard a grave divine say, that God has two dwellings, one in heaven, and the other in a meek and thankful heart.

Izaak Walton

*D*ear Lord, thank you...
For my wife so kind, so sweet,
For my family, our friends we greet,
For understanding and fun that comes our way,
For bringing gladness into each day.
For giving me honest work to do,
For allowing me to turn to You,
For shouldering my awesome cares,
For the gifts of joy the family shares,
For prayer—a talk between you and me,
It's all so good, it comes from Thee.

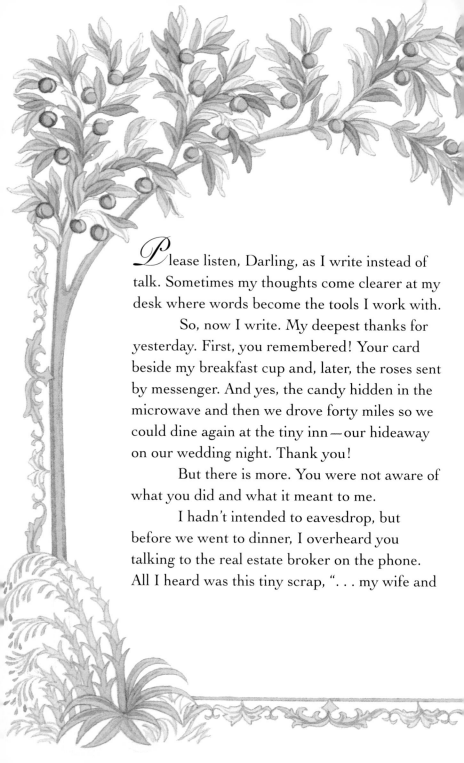

$\mathcal{P}$lease listen, Darling, as I write instead of talk. Sometimes my thoughts come clearer at my desk where words become the tools I work with.

So, now I write. My deepest thanks for yesterday. First, you remembered! Your card beside my breakfast cup and, later, the roses sent by messenger. And yes, the candy hidden in the microwave and then we drove forty miles so we could dine again at the tiny inn—our hideaway on our wedding night. Thank you!

But there is more. You were not aware of what you did and what it meant to me.

I hadn't intended to eavesdrop, but before we went to dinner, I overheard you talking to the real estate broker on the phone. All I heard was this tiny scrap, ". . . my wife and

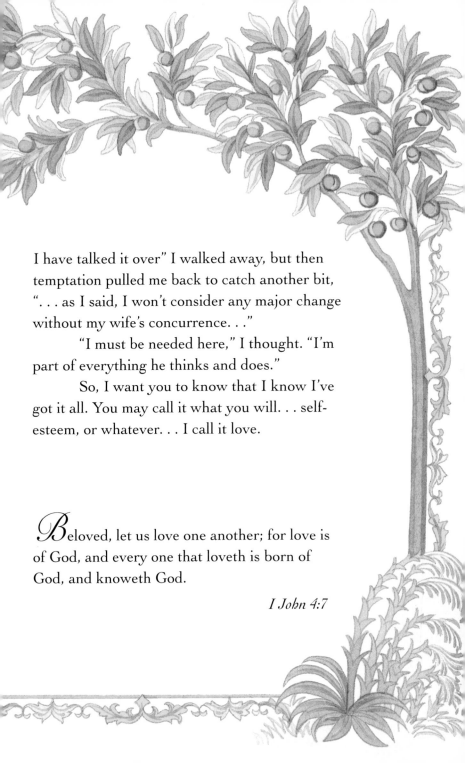

I have talked it over" I walked away, but then temptation pulled me back to catch another bit, ". . . as I said, I won't consider any major change without my wife's concurrence. . ."

"I must be needed here," I thought. "I'm part of everything he thinks and does."

So, I want you to know that I know I've got it all. You may call it what you will. . . self-esteem, or whatever. . . I call it love.

𝓑eloved, let us love one another; for love is of God, and every one that loveth is born of God, and knoweth God.

I John 4:7

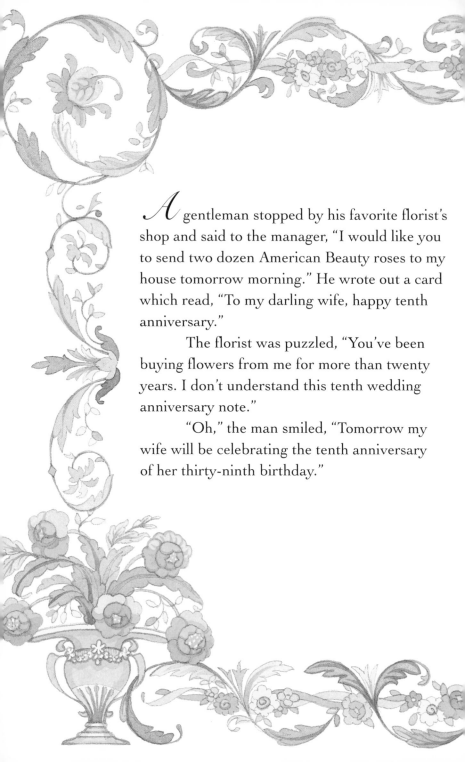

A gentleman stopped by his favorite florist's shop and said to the manager, "I would like you to send two dozen American Beauty roses to my house tomorrow morning." He wrote out a card which read, "To my darling wife, happy tenth anniversary."

The florist was puzzled, "You've been buying flowers from me for more than twenty years. I don't understand this tenth wedding anniversary note."

"Oh," the man smiled, "Tomorrow my wife will be celebrating the tenth anniversary of her thirty-ninth birthday."

To watch the corn grow, or the blossoms set, to draw hard breath over the ploughshare or spade, to read, to think, to love, to pray, are the things that make men happy.

John Ruskin

There is no remedy for love but to love more.

Henry David Thoreau

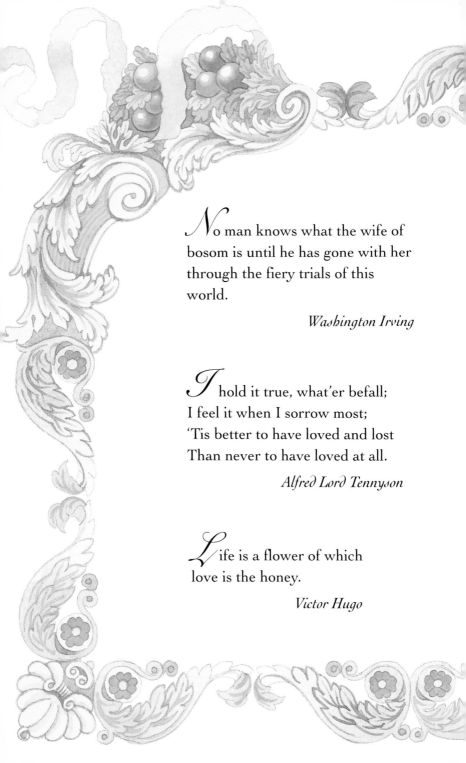

*N*o man knows what the wife of bosom is until he has gone with her through the fiery trials of this world.

Washington Irving

I hold it true, what'er befall;
I feel it when I sorrow most;
'Tis better to have loved and lost
Than never to have loved at all.

Alfred Lord Tennyson

*L*ife is a flower of which love is the honey.

Victor Hugo

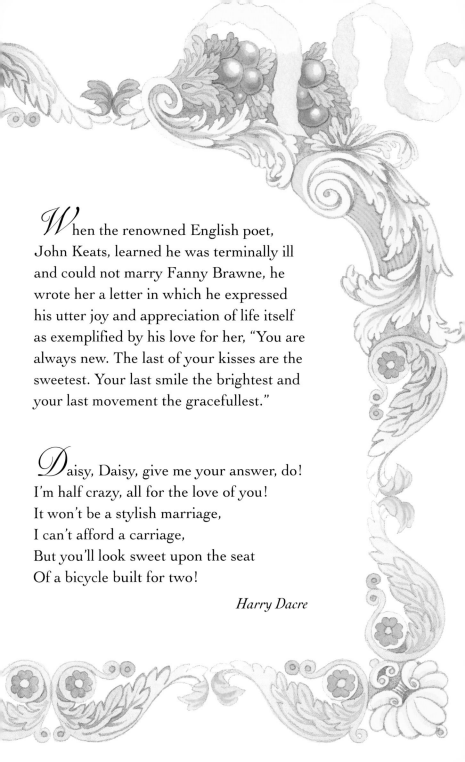

When the renowned English poet, John Keats, learned he was terminally ill and could not marry Fanny Brawne, he wrote her a letter in which he expressed his utter joy and appreciation of life itself as exemplified by his love for her, "You are always new. The last of your kisses are the sweetest. Your last smile the brightest and your last movement the gracefullest."

Daisy, Daisy, give me your answer, do!
I'm half crazy, all for the love of you!
It won't be a stylish marriage,
I can't afford a carriage,
But you'll look sweet upon the seat
Of a bicycle built for two!

Harry Dacre

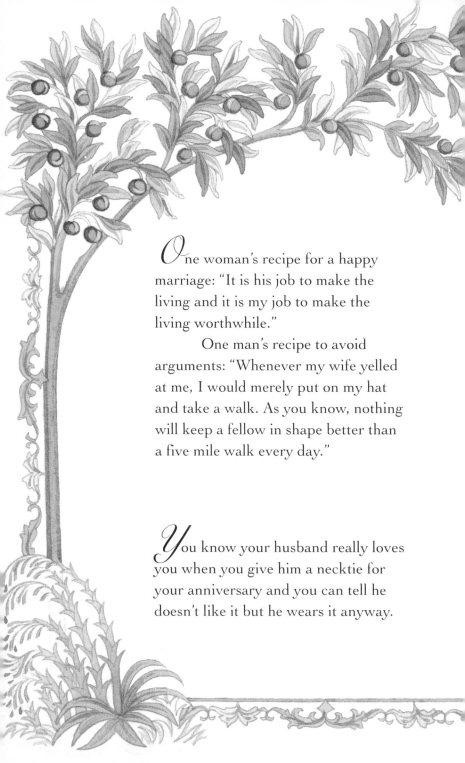

One woman's recipe for a happy marriage: "It is his job to make the living and it is my job to make the living worthwhile."

One man's recipe to avoid arguments: "Whenever my wife yelled at me, I would merely put on my hat and take a walk. As you know, nothing will keep a fellow in shape better than a five mile walk every day."

You know your husband really loves you when you give him a necktie for your anniversary and you can tell he doesn't like it but he wears it anyway.

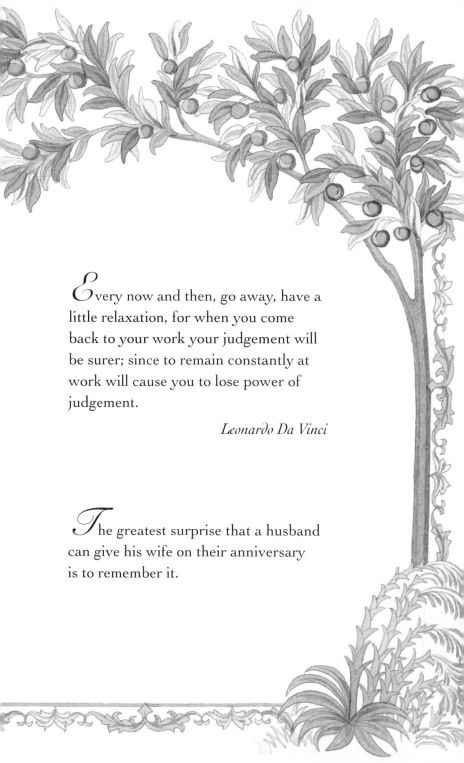

*E*very now and then, go away, have a little relaxation, for when you come back to your work your judgement will be surer; since to remain constantly at work will cause you to lose power of judgement.

Leonardo Da Vinci

*T*he greatest surprise that a husband can give his wife on their anniversary is to remember it.

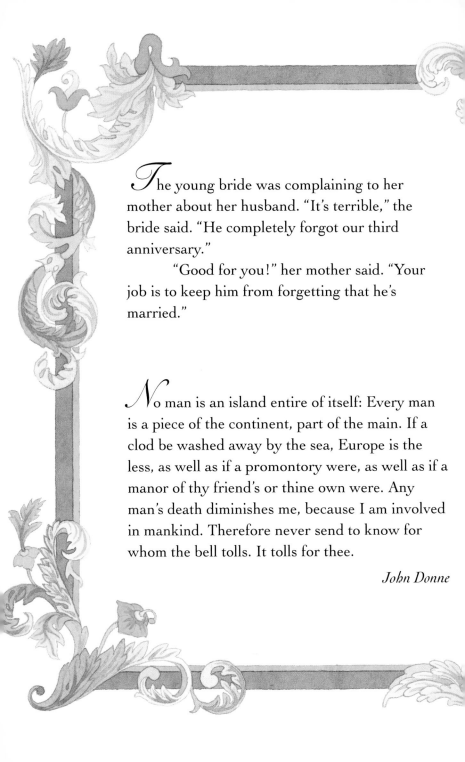

The young bride was complaining to her mother about her husband. "It's terrible," the bride said. "He completely forgot our third anniversary."

"Good for you!" her mother said. "Your job is to keep him from forgetting that he's married."

No man is an island entire of itself: Every man is a piece of the continent, part of the main. If a clod be washed away by the sea, Europe is the less, as well as if a promontory were, as well as if a manor of thy friend's or thine own were. Any man's death diminishes me, because I am involved in mankind. Therefore never send to know for whom the bell tolls. It tolls for thee.

John Donne

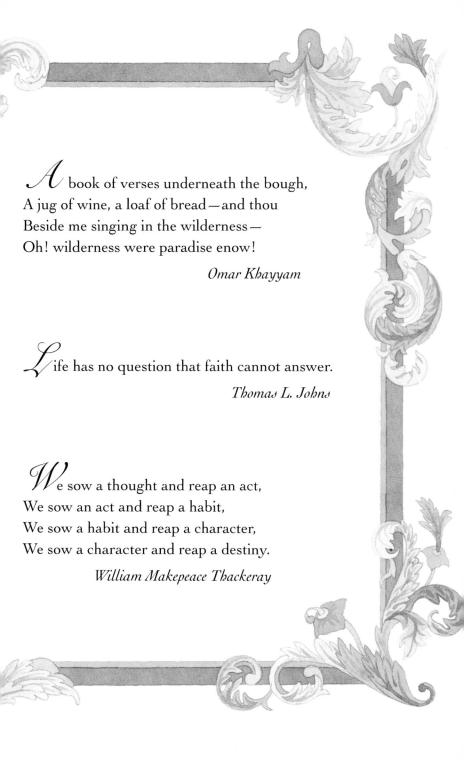

A book of verses underneath the bough,
A jug of wine, a loaf of bread—and thou
Beside me singing in the wilderness—
Oh! wilderness were paradise enow!

Omar Khayyam

*L*ife has no question that faith cannot answer.

Thomas L. Johns

*W*e sow a thought and reap an act,
We sow an act and reap a habit,
We sow a habit and reap a character,
We sow a character and reap a destiny.

William Makepeace Thackeray

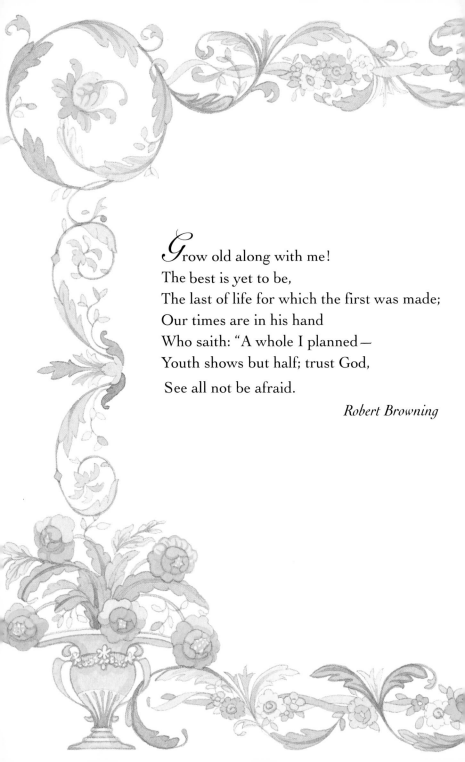

Grow old along with me!
The best is yet to be,
The last of life for which the first was made;
Our times are in his hand
Who saith: "A whole I planned—
Youth shows but half; trust God,
See all not be afraid.

Robert Browning

Dear friend,

Let's share some memories. . . sitting in that wooden swing under the oaks in the front yard of your old home down the street. . . eight years old, barefoot, hand in hand on the sandy beach. . . senior prom. . . suddenly we were grown up. You married and moved away.

We've chatted in the intervening years. . . we've shared our ups-and-downs of marriage. Now, though still so many miles separate us, I smother you with hugs. Happy Anniversary, dear old friend.

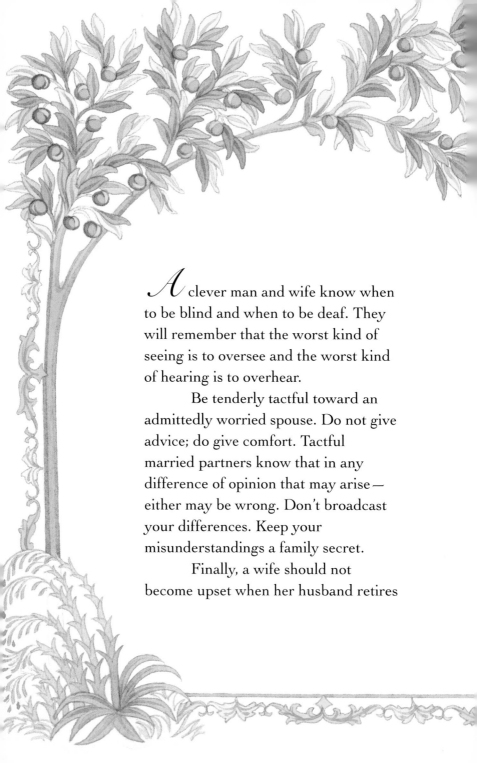

A clever man and wife know when to be blind and when to be deaf. They will remember that the worst kind of seeing is to oversee and the worst kind of hearing is to overhear.

Be tenderly tactful toward an admittedly worried spouse. Do not give advice; do give comfort. Tactful married partners know that in any difference of opinion that may arise— either may be wrong. Don't broadcast your differences. Keep your misunderstandings a family secret.

Finally, a wife should not become upset when her husband retires

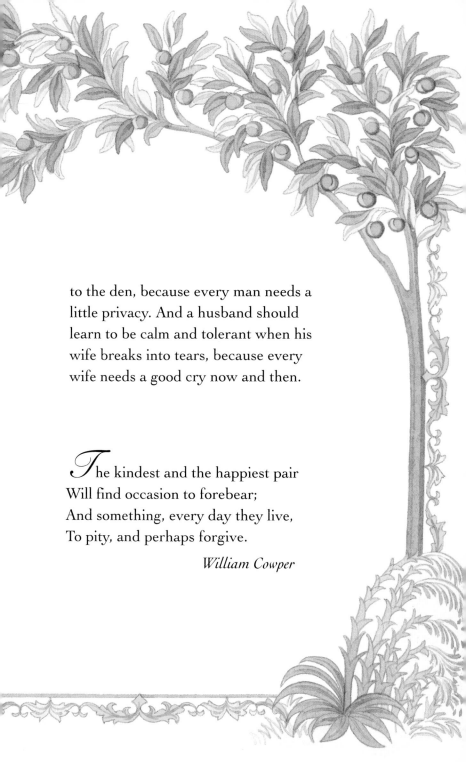

to the den, because every man needs a little privacy. And a husband should learn to be calm and tolerant when his wife breaks into tears, because every wife needs a good cry now and then.

*T*he kindest and the happiest pair
Will find occasion to forebear;
And something, every day they live,
To pity, and perhaps forgive.

William Cowper

*I*f you wish success in life, make perseverance your bosom friend, experience your wise counselor, conscience your older brother, and hope your guardian genius.

Joseph Addison

*T*here is nothing holier in this life of ours than the first consciousness of love—the first fluttering of its silken wings—the first rising sound and breath of that wind which is so soon to sweep through the soul.

Henry Wadsworth Longfellow

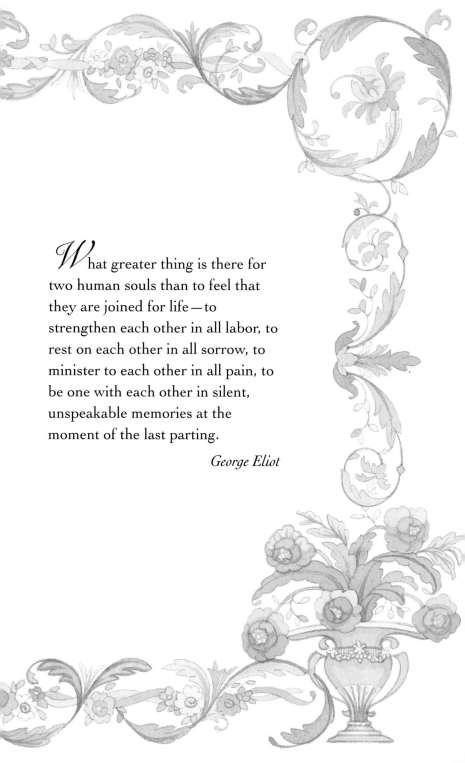

*W*hat greater thing is there for two human souls than to feel that they are joined for life—to strengthen each other in all labor, to rest on each other in all sorrow, to minister to each other in all pain, to be one with each other in silent, unspeakable memories at the moment of the last parting.

George Eliot

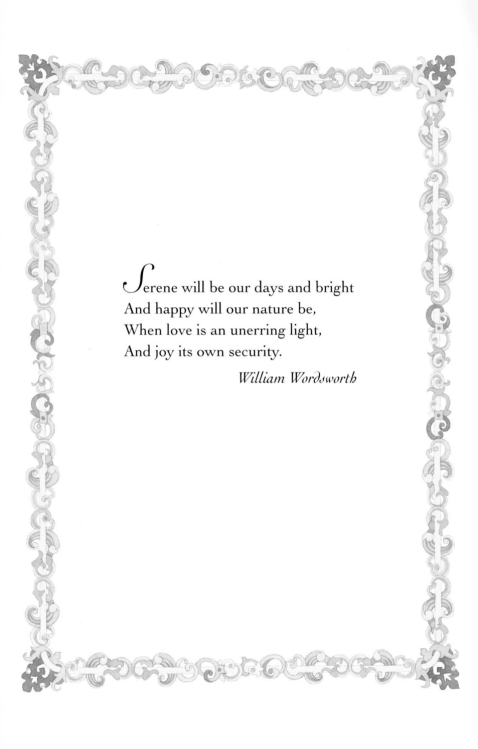

$\mathcal{S}$erene will be our days and bright
And happy will our nature be,
When love is an unerring light,
And joy its own security.

William Wordsworth